YOUR BODY AT ITS GROSSEST

SWEAT!

By Anthony Capicola

Gareth Stevens
PUBLISHING

Please visit our website, www.garethstevens.com. For a free color catalog of all our high-quality books, call toll free 1-800-542-2595 or fax 1-877-542-2596.

Cataloging-in-Publication Data

Names: Capicola, Anthony.
Title: Sweat! / Anthony Capicola.
Description: New York : Gareth Stevens Publishing, 2018. | Series: Your body at its grossest | Includes index.
Identifiers: ISBN 9781482464764 (pbk.) | ISBN 9781482464788 (library bound) | ISBN 9781482464771 (6 pack)
Subjects: LCSH: Sweat glands–Juvenile literature. | Perspiration–Juvenile literature.
Classification: LCC QP221.C37 2018 | DDC 612.7'93–dc23

Published in 2018 by
Gareth Stevens Publishing
111 East 14th Street, Suite 349
New York, NY 10003

Designer: Sarah Liddell
Editor: Ryan Nagelhout

Photo credits: Cover, p. 1 Gregory Johnston/Shutterstock.com; background gradient used throughout rubikscubefreak/Shutterstock.com; background bubbles used throughout ISebyl/Shutterstock.com; p. 5 Dinah Landry/Shutterstock.com; p. 7 Andrea Danti/Shutterstock.com; p. 9 WIRACHAIPHOTO/Shutterstock.com; p. 11 Jorg Hackemann/Shutterstock.com; p. 13 nortongo/Shutterstock.com; p. 15 MIA Studio/Shutterstock.com; p. 17 CREATISTA/Shutterstock.com; p. 19 VGstockstudio/Shutterstock.com; p. 21 Blend Images/Shutterstock.com.

Printed in China

CPSIA compliance information: Batch #CS17GS: For further information contact Gareth Stevens, New York, New York at 1-800-542-2595.

CONTENTS

Boldface words appear in the glossary.

Work It Out

Do you ever get sweaty? It probably happens after you run around or if you're at the beach on a warm day. Does it ever make you stinky? You might think sweat is gross, but it's important. Your body needs to sweat!

On the Skin

Sweat is a liquid that comes out of tiny holes in your skin called pores. Sweat is made in **glands** called eccrine (EH-kruhn) glands. Doctors have a special word for sweat: perspiration (puhrs-puh-RAY-shun). When you perspire, your eccrine glands are making a lot of sweat!

PORES

ECCRINE GLAND

7

Why Does It Happen?

Your body must be a certain **temperature** to work the right way. When it gets too warm, it must cool down. This is why we sweat! Your brain tells your body to make sweat. Your sweat cools your body as it **evaporates** from your skin.

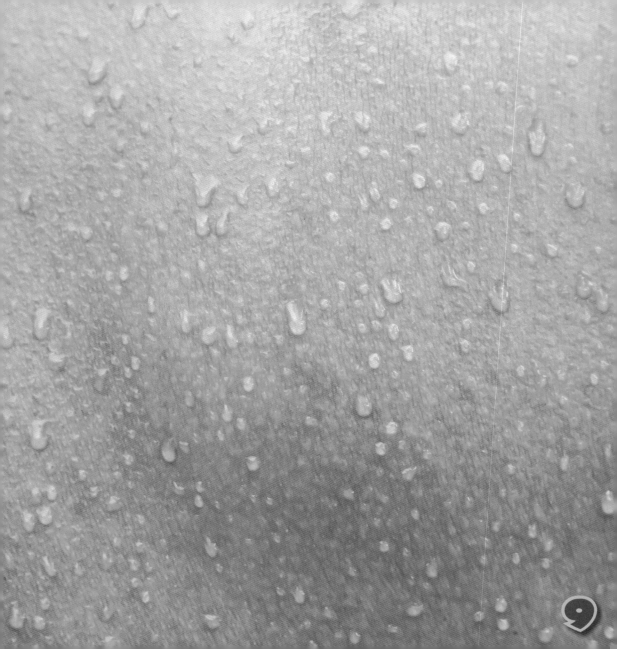

What's in It?

If you've ever been sweaty, you won't be surprised to learn sweat is mostly made of water. But it's not just water. It has some salts, sugars, and other **chemicals** in it, too.

WHAT MAKES UP SWEAT?

WATER

SALT

AMMONIA
(UH-MOH-NYUH)

SUGARS

UREA
(YUH-REE-UH)

11

Drink Up!

When you sweat, your body loses a lot of water. You need to put water back into your body, or you might get **dehydrated** (dee-HY-dray-tuhd). Drink lots of liquids and maybe eat something salty to keep your body happy!

13

Wet and Worried

Do you start to sweat when you're nervous or **stressed** about something? That's a different kind of sweat! It's made in different glands, called apocrine (AA-puh-kruhn) glands. These are only found in certain parts of your body, such as under your arms.

Stress Sweat

Your body makes stress sweat because of a **hormone** called adrenaline (uh-DREH-nuh-luhn). It's the same hormone that makes your body more **alert** and ready to act when something scary happens. Stress sweat has fats and **proteins** that make a bad smell!

Sweat Signals

Scientists aren't sure why the body makes stress sweat. Some think stress sweat is a signal, or sign, for other people. When we smell body odors from others, we might know they're nervous or that something is wrong!

Deodorant or Doctor

If you want to sweat less—or smell less—try some **deodorant** (dee-OH-duh-ruhnt). But sometimes people sweat too much. This is called hyperhidrosis (hy-puhr-hy-DROH-suhs). If you think you sweat a lot, see a doctor. But remember, most sweat is good!

GLOSSARY

alert: being watchful and ready to meet danger

chemical: matter that can be mixed with other matter to cause changes

dehydrate: to lose water and other bodily liquids

deodorant: something that blocks bad smells

evaporate: to change from a liquid to a gas

gland: a body part that produces something needed for a bodily function

hormone: something made in the body that tells another part of the body what to do

protein: a necessary element found in all living things

stress: a state of concern, worry, or feeling nervous

temperature: how hot or cold something is

FOR MORE INFORMATION

BOOKS

Barnhill, Kelly Regan. *The Sweaty Book of Sweat.* Mankato, MN: Capstone Press, 2010.

Claybourne, Anna. *Smelly Farts and Other Body Horrors.* New York, NY: Crabtree Publishing Company, 2015.

WEBSITES

Smelly Sweat
cyh.com/HealthTopics/HealthTopicDetailsKids.aspx?p=335&np=152&id=2961
Visit this site to find out why sweat smells.

What's Sweat?
kidshealth.org/en/kids/sweat.html
Learn more here about why you sweat and what it means.

INDEX